FOR THE BEAUTY OF THE EARTH
AF333641
Loving Our World by Lorraine Capparell

For Peggy Siok Hui, Ravissimo, Linda, Raj, Nathan, and Vijay,
who made so many happy memories at Pertama.

With special thanks to
Carmanita in Jakarta
and Jagdev in Malaysia.

Oruwa fishing boat, Mirissa, Sri Lanka

For the Beauty of the Earth

Douglas Bullis

ATELIER BOOKS LTD.CO.

Contents

I saw the last sunshaft of yellow
off the flowers in a garden,
felt the shamal wind
prowl air's cactus night.
The world is dying
for the peoples in this book.
So what's the worth of our MFAs,
art openings,
Collected Works,
which feed no child, no soul, no tribe, no future?
If this is the end of their era on the Earth,
have our sunflowers become more wrinkled than autumns?
Can we finally go beyond the pretty contrivances,
the perfect plot structures,
the fool's gold of fame,
the how-to books for writers crying for stardom
who never cried for lives foreign, faraway, and poor?
Can we seek worthier truths
than our surfeiting world fritters
with the toylings of economy?
Skrælings to our own motives,
is it not the time we have long seen coming,
to turn the tiller on joft seas,
toward those such as the Badui people of West Java
who know truth's survival better than we:
"Our planet is our body,
its water our blood
its air our breath
its fire our spirit
its fate our wind.
We are it;
it is not us." *

* Quote courtesy of Carmanita in Jakarta.

Thousand-year-old olive, still producing, Agia Anna Byzantine chapel,
Koufalotos, Crete

There Is a Tree in Time

There is a tree in time in which there are two beings.
They live there, hand to hand from leap to fruit.
When the storm comes they cower
amid the boughs of thick leaves.

There, in the vast majesty of distance,
in the sun and the wind and the dusk and the summer,
they see a light that is endless,
a light that is an essence,
a brilliance
a radiance
a sun.

Then the sky clears and they descend onto the plains.
The sun is warm there and they hold up their arms and run free,
naming sun gods, sky gods, myths, the paths of planets.
When the storm comes they are far from the tree, and cower.

Then the sky clears and like pillars the names rise,
linears and labyrinths into cities of vertices.
When the storm comes they cower,
peer out from their windows
dreaming of summer in a tent under a tree.

39 Steps Waterfall, Hogsback, South Africa

Shi yen i

Leaves fall
plangent roars
amid my footsteps faint along the wilderness path.
In those dry and curling remains of fallen ideas,
do I see beauty veiled in the mist
or is the veil a disguise?
Do the rising wolves of the pathwayed world
live the illusions I embrace
because I have none of my own?
Or am I really, unknown even to my mirror,
makyo,
the delusions that give rise to illusions,
that each by each we one day see
behind the energy diameters of all our confusions,
hallucinogens of Self that O!
would that we might become wise
by knowing the link of the two.
And, too, accept the verso side in me,
who pulls the puppet threads of I the fool,
the shallow vanity of my bourgeois *blaggarderie*
the pathetic triteness of the art on my walls
all for lacking the temerity
to ask someone who knows more than I.
Why, when I cry, does the water in my eyes
cleanse neither sky nor soul?

Am I Sungchil from Haein-sa?
Sungchil
who was famed for his daily practice of 3,000 prostrations
which required seven hours

and to those many who came to him for counsel
he said he would receive them
only when they had done 3,000 prostrations
for each of the 108 beads of Afflicted States.
Many were angry
and set off to find an easier savior
but those who did the 3,000 prostrations
for each of the 108 beads
found they no longer needed him.
These told others
and soon the entirety of Haein-sa
commenced to live the *Metta Sutta.*
He lived to ninety-six
and when he died
the perfections of his province
died with him.

Am I the tall slender woman in the corner café,
so thin she seems but a wift of sticks
moving to the gusts of will,
wearing a red-and-white tiny-patterned houndstooth shirt
with the tail hanging out from the waist of her jeans,
hair a ragmop of once-blond looks,
face as plaited as the love knot of the Scots,
eyes of near-majestic nonengagement,
body shape now lost into the bones
of her life's grand succession
from needle to needle and spoon to spoon
and yet a shape that
upon closer look
ascends and descends her Sisyphean day
like a great and stately staircased building
reaching the top only to descend
reaching the bottom only to ascend
perceptible only by her ghostly progress of shadows,

up and down and up and down,
whose physicality has long been lost
into the great wandering search for salvation
yearning out of her eyes.

Hasn't it been enough to filter sand
through the decisions of your fingers
as through an hourglass
and watch it turn to rain to feathers to leaves
to diamonds to faces out of the past
to a woman haloed with fishes which
upon closer look are in fact doves
to tales told by children
in the ascendancy of the schoolyard
to the chatterbox expulsiveness of a man
who has no idea how full of himself he is
Oxbridge Ph.D. and all
to the dunes of nudes in auto sculpture
glimpsed in a too-bright sun
while the roadsides of yellow-bright rose bushes
wither fume by fume into a lacework forest
dark at dawn on a moist spring morning
to the history stamens of *kabuki*
hiding in Elizabethan slashed sleeves,
all of these all of these revealing the silk within all beings
which by glimpses and only by glimpses
is more enduring and empowering
than by whole cloth
just as is the woman who boudoirs herself perfectly
reveals more by what is not seen than by what is,
to the ever-presence of time flying,
to your meanders through old family photo albums
discovering of a sudden every origin
of what you once were
and you are horrified

by what lay in the background of those images
that at the time you never noticed
was far more interesting than you,
to the bound goat in the cave
behind which the cookfires begin
and in your goat mind you wonder
why aren't they afraid of that flicker?
It's hot.

exeunt

Exeunt via the timelines
of your Gordian knot
your loop of folds and entwinings
and colors more than rainbows
turning ever more majestic
as you fathom the mysteries of linkage
between all this and all as yet undreamed
till in a searing instant you are severed by a sword
and your mind of visions falls away to the earth
on which your sand of wonder once flowed
and you gaze up in a single last glimpse
at the man in metal armor
turning to the next just like you
and you say
why did you cut me?
I was only the beauty to be found
in a grain of sand with a mind of its own.

exeunt

Or am I Navagunavala
the nine sublimities of the *Tathagata*
the thus-come-thus-gone ephemera
of life which is self but not-self
to the finely crocheted cotton monkeyfists of the Burmese

which are then varnished till they become beads
on the *mani* of Asia's rosaries.
Of what use is ephemera
unless it ignites phorescence?
Am I the width of the moon multiplied by its distance
or the distance to the sun divided by the sun's width?
Both are 108.
Does that revelation come from phorescence, too?

exeunt

Or am I the clothes
the accent
and the miserable cassette tapes
offered by a retired civil servant
who is trying to sell his three
scratched
dirty
obviously unplayable
collections of Parsi folk songs
now locked into immobility
by their days in a Bombay street gutter
spotted by the desperate eye
of a man whose fixed pension
is slowly becoming worthless
as inflation and all else rises
and sells anything he can get his hands on
for the price of a meal?
Would you treat him to a few hours of respite
by way of a *shawmala* vendor
in a streetcorner hawker stall,
a *shawmala* pita cone
filled with slices of broiled chicken
fried potatoes
minced cabbage
pickled beet

mayonnaise,
all rolled carefully to be eaten like an ice-cream cornet?
Or am I the you in your you
who would buy him that *shawmala* if only
you could be there at the right place and right time?

exeunt

Am I the urchin beggars fake and real,
the flute seller who doesn't sing much better than his flutes
a cigarette hawker voicing an emphysemic *bzzzlaaghhh*
the untouchable *dalits* manifesting out of nothing
from after midnight till before dawn
scavenging into the filthy jute bags
slung over their shoulders
every potentially vendable scrap and remnant
of civilization's detritus
left after the close of the day?

exeunt

Or am I
as you contemplate your own world's cruel mix
of the ghastly and the noble
a shoemender
whose entire premises
is his lap
and a box at each knee
who serves a steady stream of those
with soles in need of cementing
or laces that require replacing
and who has condensed his entire income stream
into one tube of glue
and fifty or so shoelaces
from the girlishly colorful
to the businessy mundane

all of which are properly knotted
around a slim stub of wood
so you see right there
exactly what you're going to wear,
and who from this establishment-in-a-lap,
has put his four children through
the best schools his caste allows
children who
when their maturity matches his dotage
will support him through his accelerating debilities?

exeunt

As Master Kung put it,
"Writing, *shi,*
cannot fully express the meaning of speech, *yen;*
speech cannot express the full meaning of ideas, *i.*"
And when a student asked
if anyone could understand the sages,
Master Kung replied,
"The sages established the images, *hsiang,*
to express the meaning of their ideas;
they devised the diagrams, *kua,*
to express the distinction between true and false;
and they attached judgments, *tz'u,*
in order to fully express their speech."

Utter them as one: *shi yen i hsiang kua tz'u—*
how lyric sound the syllables
that bind us ever to approximation.

Think of the confusions of our temporary existences
the dilemmas of which way to turn
on the pathway's necklace of uncountable pearls,
fusillading as we do from the bang of our beginning
simply to ask, "From what does our universe derive?

A self knowing itself?
Lightning bolt from the gods?
Touch of a finger from father to son
painted into permanence above the stinging eyes
of a man cursed to his labors?
From trimonotintinnabulation
the sound of a single bell rung thrice that begins *zazen?*
From Descartes' dadodecadodefibrillihedron
the geometric figure
that merges shape with law
and of these makes meaning?"

Or am I
in the hope you always have been
and do not yet know

you?

Settlement Village, South Africa

n'Fnaa

Greatness should not write its history.
Centuries are better scribes.

I am the grandfather of ancestors.
I am before Picasso, Matisse, Van Gogh discovered me.
I am before borders clutched me.
I am before fictions falsified me.
I am before cities bewitched away the children of my villages.
I am before murder was legalized by flags on a pole.
I am before bronze, iron, swords, armies,
from which no user is innocent of what they do to the living.
I am before anthropology professors
turned their lenses upon my artifacts
inspected my minutiae,
ignored my magnitude,
concluded what they wanted to conclude,
without the bother of living with me
as I live with myself,
to see if their words were true.
I am extended articles in costly journals
lecturing one another
without first asking my cess.
If they had they would learn
that the paper on which their learning stales
upon publication of the next issue
comes from my villages which awakened one morning
to hacked and bulldozed forests,
that turned my fields into mud now yielding wan harvests.

I read their pages,
listen to their words,
and I ask, Where are my trees, where are my villages?
How silent are their learned papers then.

Words.
Vast muscle-show vocabularies of them
so void of my tribe and clan and family,
the wellsprings of my being,
I wonder if they know
what a humanity is.
With my heart open,
my eyes look into theirs
and I ask why being dark skinned
buries my humanity under faceless footnotes
of *ipso facto quod vide prima facie ibid quid pro quo op cit exemplia grata.*
You have dictionaries,
I have life.
It flows in me, spills from me, breathes in me,
begets my urge to endure
while vocabularies beget but vocabularies.

Then came the coffee-table books
fat with pretty pictures of my surfaces,
packaged, parceled, focus grouped, page designed, test marketed;
They photoshopped my eyes off the pages,
took no pictures of my love, my anger, my bewonderment
at the passing night's starry messengers.
They chose pictures of my cookpots, my huts, my colored cloth,
my scarifications, dances, ceremonies,
everything but how my children are cared for.
The pretty pictures piqued interest in my artifacts
by calling them art,
and I soon saw my works of cloth,
so meaningful to me,
begaud instead fashion models and catwalk fantasies,

who understood nothing of its texture,
its feel on the skin, its fragrance,
and how the soul in the loom
never makes the same piece twice.
My village found its way diorama'd in miniature
into anthropology departments,
where my ancestry was sanitized,
denuded of tribe,
stripped of my children, my suckling women,
the *wss-wss-wsses* of gossip that spread like wind,
the sounds under the moon of child-making's hopes,
the sky above and earth below,
in which I both fear and take comfort.
The sumtotal of all these erasures and scrubbings and whitewash
ended on shelves with other books just like the first,
half the world and time-out-of-mind away
from the dusty, child-filled, fly-laden, charcoal-cooking,
feasting/starving/dance-making village
where my artifacts were made
and me with them.

We awoke one morning
to find our elder-law pushed aside by writ-law
and suddenly found ourselves
colonized, Christianized, and consumerized.
The morning after we awakened to our worship shrines
stripped as bare as our fields
when the ancient gods living in the sacredness of our trees
were chopped down for floor coverings, hangers, and party chairs.
Then came the dealers and collectors
(our world now being safe and tidy enough for them to enter)
with certificates of sale we could not read.
Thumbprint by thumbprint and X by Y and Y by Z,
what remained of our art
vanished into museums and foyers,
entrances to executive suites, art galleries,

mansions, magazines, and luxury shops,
none of which would we be permitted to enter,
while face by face, child by child, textile by textile,
we desiccated in the wind now withering our villages.

My greatness is within, not without.
I have my heart and my skin and my soul.
No one can loot me into less.
Now behold me as I am to myself,
for in memory of these I shall never die—

I am the carved wood latch from a granary door
surmounted by a simply shaped sheaf of barley
smoothed by time-unconcerned decades of hands.
In the seeing of this
you see how much of my art, and therefore myself,
was of a practical nature
too busy for the traps of prestige.
See my hands in the cotton-combing blocks, drums,
looms, boxes, axe handles, mallets, dishes, cups,
spoons, mortars, pestles, combs, beads,
headrests, canoes, paddles, toys?
All carved by spare-time talent
apprenticed at age seven to uncles,
and who in due time acquired mastery, too,
thence to carve in their turn for needy neighbors,
because in making something necessary
for the welfare of a neighbor
artisanship transcends the self.

Now Ifa bowl from Nigeria am I
the size of two salad bowls,
one inverted base to base on the other.
The waist between these halves
is a banded frieze of carved figures—
a drummer, a farmer, a tiller, a house-sweeper,
a grain-pounder, a fly-whisker, a fecund mother of three,

a buxom young bride, a dancer, a child,
a jaunty grinning simpleton on a bicycle;
altogether sixteen.
At first these look like a storyboard,
those plots with no words carved onto planks
that village tale-tellers rely upon
to recall a legend's main points
while they curlicue word blossoms in all directions,
turning thereby each story and every teller
into a tale of himself
hiding inside the wood.
In hushed auction rooms
I am described as nicely decorated, straightforward, functional.
How little they realize
in the frieze is the soul of a dead *griot*
given perpetual life by the soul in the wood.
Starvation in lean years,
feasts in fruited years,
once depicted on a bit of wood
ne'er forgot and somehow still living.
Ownership turns my people into things;
lost are the characters, faces, villages,
wives, sons, daughters, cows, pigs,
recited by a quavering voice
in a fireside huddle
with a dark storm flashing behind our backs,
all suddenly extinguished
when the auction gavel claps the bowl's demise.
All the lives depicted on that banded frieze,
all our memories made one,
the weather, the wind, the annual rains,
the life of desert and death
of all days past
and all days destined.

Vanished.
Forever.

The bowl's lifetime duty was to preserve them all,
progeny one, progeny many,
giving nourishment to our return.
Turn this bowl in your hands.
Soar your eyes over the sixteen figures
whose personas are one in many and many in one,
reflecting my hundreds of gods,
each with its own music, songs, rhythm, dance,
all under Olorun the sky god, who guides our destinies
but withdraws in the presence of lesser gods with louder voices.
This pot held sixteen palm nuts,
food for Ifa the god of divination
whose hunger is sated through our shaman
who alone among us knows the proper nut on the palm to pluck.
To our nut gathering which nourished the spirit
came people with bell, book, and candle,
who forbade our Ifa's worship
and have you not noticed how starved now are our villages?
A nut without its god is not even food.

Now Ibido am I.
Helmet mask from Nigeria.
See how much I say with so little?
Into me has been carved the unnameable mystery
beyond which we see.
The carver's hand guiding the chisel and burnisher
is the hand of our mysteries.
The collector sees a delicately modeled face,
features slightly awry, puffy eyes,
embellished circlets of hair at forehead and temples,
delicate lips, marmot-like ears, enormous headdress
of intricately carved wood thimbles,
calls it beautiful
and it is,
contemplative
and it is,
mystical

and it is that as well.
Then why are my face and my village
not beautiful and contemplative and mystical too?
Why am I not in your definitions of a soul?
Are my features not those in the mask?
How can you see in me nothing
when in your hand you hold no mere mask,
you hold everything?

Now Yoruba am I.
Into my villages are born many twins.
Often one sees not the end of its first year.
The mother deems the village carver to shape her a figure
with the same face as the child.
She cares for this carving
as if the face carved into it is still alive.
She decorates it with anklets and bead necklaces,
plaits its hair after braiding the surviving child's hair,
puts it to one breast while feeding with the other.
In the end she handles it so often
the original coarse features gleam
as polished ebony.
Do you not, knowing this,
want to hold the mother as she holds her dead child
still alive in this wood?
Do you not feel within yourself
the power of love that keeps life going
before it has come
till after it has gone?
Our humanity is her humanity,
there is in each of us so much of it.

Salvation light to caravans too was I,
all the way from Tagháza to Walata, some 500 miles,
broken by but one oasis.
So barren this land,
so unremarkable of landmark,

so easy the chance of becoming lost,
that between survival instinct and my trader's eyes
begat the idea of relief caravan bearing naught but water and food.
I sent my Musafa desert hunters ahead
to inform the merchants of Walata of our coming.
We dispatched into the desert night
our water-bearing camels,
for by then after forty days
the merchants would be very short of water,
if not depleted to the last camel-skin flask.
Who can count the number of cries I heard over the centuries
showering Allah's praises
when the men on the trek saw our torches atop the camels
blink over the horizon?
Such a clamor it was!
To them we were Allah's merciful salvation,
brighter even than the brightest stars.
When we heard their great cry
of "*Aid!*" "*Succor!*" "*Allahu Akbar!*"
faint in the distance yet louder than the wind,
we knew which stars to guide by
for beneath them were men joyously weeping.
Yes, I did that,
centuries of it,
and you ask if I be not proud?

Now music am I,
great, joyous, lamenting, celebrating, weeping, lovestruck arcs of it,
on my right from Senegal to Congo
and on my left from Somalia to the southernmost cape
'round which your great ships passed from your world into mine,
and from mine to worlds beyond.
Gold from my mines at Bambuk and Buré sent I.
Hides, nuts, ostrich feathers,
fabrics of many kinds.

By way of reward Europe sent us its great export to the world—
artificial borders to fight over,
and arms to do it with.
How can I not mock the civilization
that so celebrates itself at home
yet leaves in foreign lands cluster bombs and disease,
hacked forests, grubbed diamonds,
seeds that grow but one crop and then die.
I kept our music, for it alone preserved our history.
From Diabate comes my sweet Malian *kora*.
From Ali Farka Touré came voice and strings so sonorous
and notes so many he could be at once
waves on the sea and sand on the desert
and you would not be able to know the one
without knowing the two.

What you know of me is what my villager knows
upon entering a city for the first time
and chancing across a necktie shop.
As he tries to imagine the garment
that goes with such an object,
you try to imagine
what he sees in the coming blue of turning sky.
As he tries to comprehend who would wear such a strange shape,
you try to comprehend the great folds of his garments,
their patterns of kuba and kinta,
why they are colored so,
why they are so wrapped.
He tries to imagine the point of wearing
so slender a bit of pattern,
you try to imagine why anyone would choose
to envelop his entire body in dazzling design and color.
He asks himself, "Where do they keep their sky gods?
Their life spirit that flies out of the cookfire?"
You ask in reply, "What is a sky god? What is a life spirit?
What is a cookfire?"

Thus the forlorn fragments of me
I have been able to clutch
inside my African mask.
Why should you care about me when all you want
is to buy and sell and show and tell?
I am this mask,
and we the both
are but a part of a whole costume,
made of beads and grass and skins and shells,
intricately assembled to distill the essence
that breathes life into my rituals.
The face behind the mask
emerges only at night,
under the moon
where hundreds of my villagers
have gathered before the flickering shadows of fires,
amid voices and drums of dance,
faces of bewondering children,
squalling babies,
smells of smoldering wood and cooking gazelle,
dogs racing through the dust,
dozen upon dozen of masks such as my own,
faces of friends now mythical beings,
bodies now spirits,
secular turning to sacred,
known becoming unknown
hopes lifted into the safety of the imaginary
as all uncertainties vanish
into the great chrondic roar
by which we shall in the end
prevail.

When, my friend,
will you hear me?

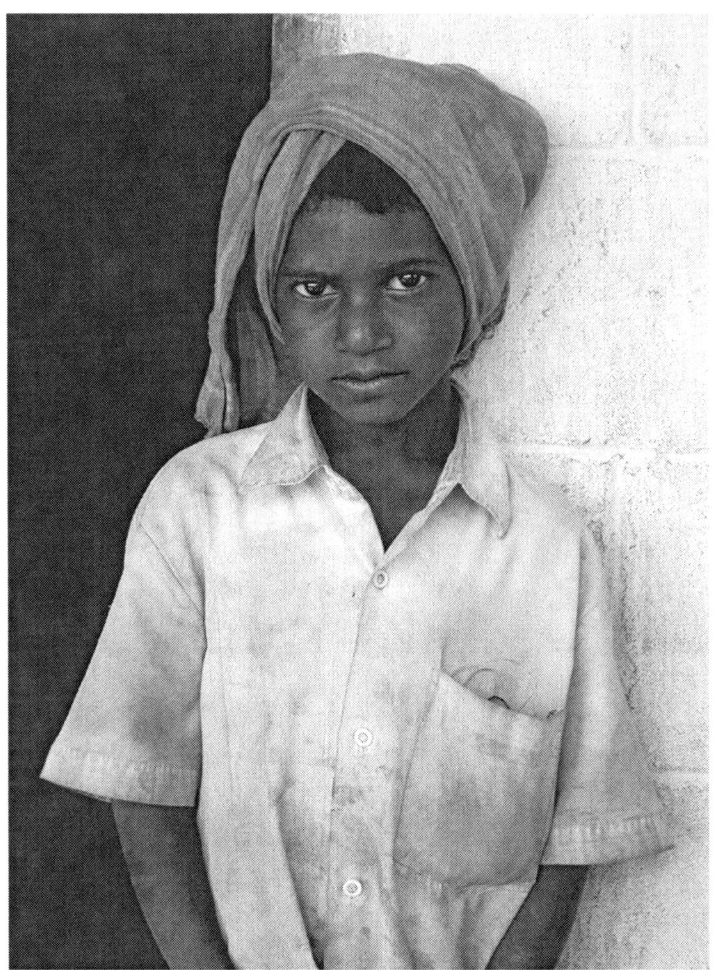

Lesotho farm boy, age 11

Fisherman's Wife

When white cirrus-stallions flail their manes in the sky
the fishing boats go leaving.
Glissades of wavelets vee back from their prows
as they clear the jetty,
tiller into the wind,
climb the
incoming
swells,
slide down
the other
side,
unerring,
into the void
beyond the sky.

Greatness and emptiness await them,
eternity, perhaps, at a pace humans can understand.
A waxing moon
drags tides out of the sea,
children out of the womb.

A woman pauses at the edge of the quay,
waves to one of the boats passing.
Her husband waves back.
Beyond the pretty harborside calm of peach-hued clouds
is a sea of no law and no mercy.
She knows this,
says it in the hesitancy of her wave.
He knows it too,
says it in his.
A gull teeters alone
on the edges of the fishing life:
the women on the quay pushing the pram,
the humdrums of the hearth,

the half a loaf uneaten,
the missing pieces of roof,
the walls needing paint,
the linger-eyed schemes of foul-weather men,
the grief unending in husband-at-sea dreams.
All in a wave.

What must it be like married to a man of the sea?
When the children were not yet born,
before the sun had tanned him into old-rope brown,
before he became tired of the daily drudge of the boat,
embittered by dwindling catches,
before he had grown obsessed with providing,
he would return urgently home,
flying the waves to her
with as much haste as the sea could provide.
How their first years must have been hurried and hopeful,
and how the hurry departed on hope's fading hours
when they spoke through the long nights
eyes open in the dark,
so unlike the eyes-open nights now,
when he is to sea.
Trembling they were then,
unquenchable passion one moment,
fathomless fear the next,
the need that he must go,
the long nights of silence
worrying how she might live as a widow.
When, in their love-flamboyant mood,

what were his words when her voice fell low
that a new bud had broken and she was with child?
Did he nod and gaze at the ground?
Did he sigh and look to sea?

When the storm season thrashes the jetty,
still he must go;
men of the sea have no will of their own.
Women say they understand,
but they know how the sky shrieks
like the airplanes above
on their missions of war.
The rain breaks the gunnels, then the mast.
When pouring ceases and the storm winds fall,
what of the hull?

In every sea are moments of hue,
moments of light,
moments of terror,
moments of wind.
The children must be told only
that Father sleeps at sea,
they who had grown so familiar
with his fatherhood hand.

'nch *Allah* that he died.
But it was not 'nch *Allah* how he died.
The airplanes came shrieking
on their missions of war.
Yellow flames took the boats.
Of fourteen that left
none returned.
The airplanes were many things,
but not 'nch *Allah.*

Shaitan!   Shaitan!   Shaitan!

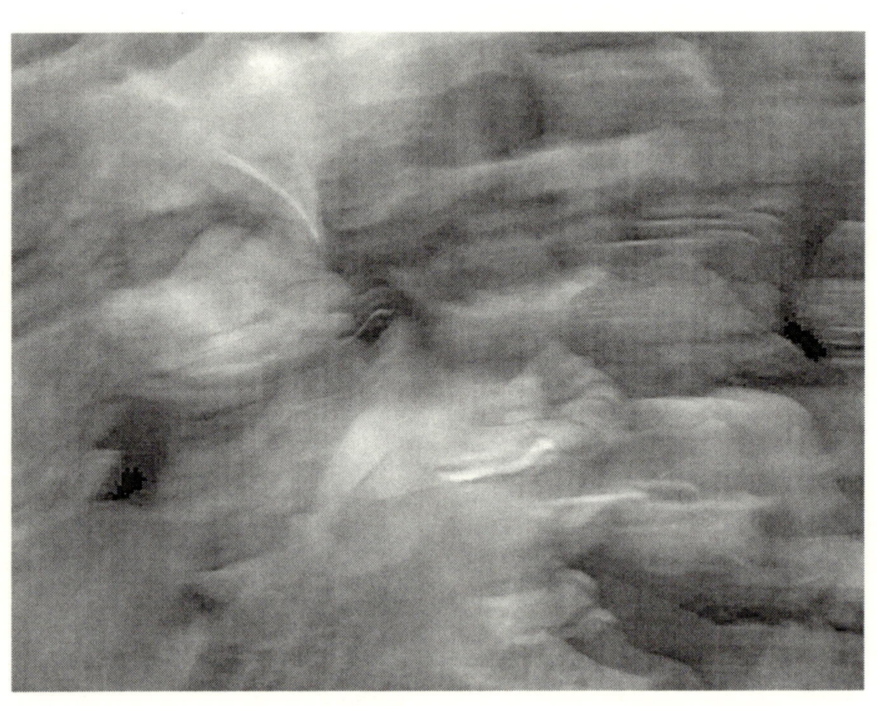

When Sikhs Dance

The Wesak or Vaishiki Festival on the May full moon is celebrated by many South and Southeast Asian societies. Among Buddhists it is a holy day that commemorates the birth, enlightenment (nibbana), and passing (parinibbana) of Gautama Buddha. Other religious and secular groups celebrate it as well, reinforcing the notion everywhere that party time is party time.

Sukhdev, Goddess of Happiness,
will-of-the-wisps across the threshold
on her first Grand Entrance ever.
She dances into evening elegance
that replaces day's wrinkles,
where earth tones mix with azures and purples.
Cast off now from day's moorings
pale blue *khameezes* mix with white silk
shoulder to wrist,
there to meet the iron bangles
that distinguish Sikh from Punjabi
inside the same bit of geography.
A sea of brown skin, bays of blue sequins,
sandbanks of saffron sleeve.
Oval smiles cascade beneath flowerfalls of black orchid hair.
Colors rich as sweets made of honey and ghee,
noses delicious as sculpted chocolate.

Chandsingh, Lion of the Moon,
old enough now to have earned his quavering voice,
eyeglasses propped up on his turban,
takes the microphone,
entreaties, "Pray together,
but if you have not the time,
have at least dinner together."

Chandkaur Princess of the Moon laments an old Punjabi love song:

I will build a home and make it a heaven for our love.
Coming into your arms I am afraid for myself.
When my eyes meet yours, I become a fish out of water,
fluttering,
fluttering.
With you I won't sing
of who I was before,
I will sing that I am
the music of a flute
that bewitches
into butterflies.
River of my life,
ocean of my love,
listen to my prayer:
My earth is empty,
let your rains come.
We are apart,
bring us together.
Take the light of my eyes
and give them your rain,
let my dry earth grow
flowers in the dry season,
let my prayer seduce the gods so I may seduce you
and with my love change this earth
into a land of flowers
*which turn my wilted leaves into fresh.**

Women conceal their beauties
with bodices falling Punjabi-style
in sheer monochrome free-falls of benthic blue.
Saffron and matte gold
on hither-eyed beauties,
flickering faces
in the candlelit procession

---

* Lyrics translated by my dear friend Jagdev of Kajang, Malaysia.

honoring the sacrament that is rice.
Crimson silk
charcoal cotton
gold brocade
Aladdin-toed shoes.
A tot of a girl in a pale yellow *khameez*
and silk skirt of marble and gold
carmel and gold
garnet and gold
cinnabar and gold
moonstone and gold
tourmaline and gold—
she, mere sky child now,
will one day emerge far-winged Sélène
goddess of the moon.

Shawls drape chastely over throats
streaming backward over the
shoulders—
angels with folded wings.
Flowing spangles and brocades
iridesce into sari-fall *osaris*
of pouring topaz.
Dance music like an accordion
on fast-forward,
so riotous it justifies a garment
of pink and tangerine tie-dye-edged with woven silver,
worn by a little girl posing as Priceless Miss Precious
for Daddy's camera.
Formerly floral ladies who frumped before their time
now dress in grays, their version of gold with no glitter.
Reds enough to envy a sunset
emerald greens and sapphire blues
black and silver laced with indigo imperiale.
The impish nonchalance of a born scene-stealer.
Vest and *shalwar* of gold-mine sequins

cloaking a *khameez*'s infathomable artistry of stripes
as if to say weft is loom's most joy-giving gift.
One woman wore a single solid hue,
an impossible-to-conjure image of rose and crimson,
neither too vermilion nor too carmine,
not quite carnelian with all of its browns,
yet neither quite cerise with its stage-whispers of black,
she was red's finest hour.

Again *Chandkaur* sang
or did the song sing her?

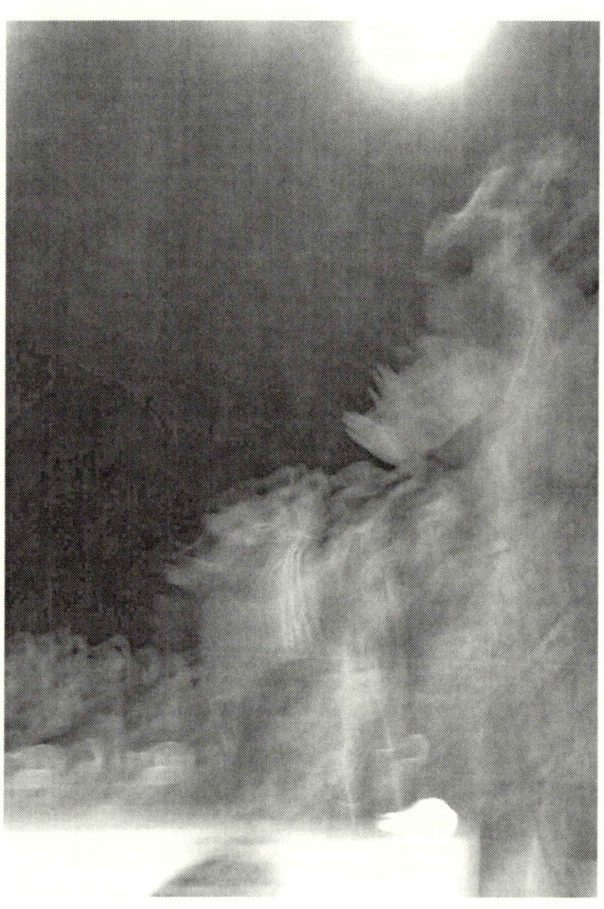

You gave me
the heartache of love
yet where are you now?
I walk the emptiness
of my desert,
every step I take
in search of you.
My night goes by
with unclosed lids;
my days are many hours
of unhappy song.
Oh love, come back,
come back to me.
Oh love, I will live
in your hut
I will come
into your arms
and yield my emptiness.
I will turn my finger
into a pen,
write these words
onto your heart:
Since you came
into my life

I'd rather be in your fate
than in the smiles of the gods.
Please, Oh my lover, my god,
come back to me
come back.

The evening's-end dance
melted into a riot of paints
no longer edged by shapes
but by the half-awake/half-asleep point
when dreamtime becomes real
and realtime becomes dream,
and both skein into a silk of woven touch
so blended with being
that life, sex, self, love,
the fire of love and chill of fate,
with its chill, too, of time and departure,
become one—

no, no,
not one.
Not a thousand and one
nor ten thousand and one
a hundred thousand and one.
Just . . . One.

It was the grandest dance an eye ever laid to.

December 26, 2004

When I last saw her
she was running
down the beach
streaming behind her
brilliant red and yellow
saris torn from some washline.
She was screaming
running
her voice wailing for everyone to hear
into the billows of the streamers
the billows of the sea
the billows of the clouds
running
screaming
as she dwindled into an arrow of color
arcing along the length of the beach
till I no longer
heard her
but I
could still see that ululation of color,
Hindu sacred saffron
Buddha-flag red,
first small
then tiny
then speck
yet still screaming the
same words
at the top of her voice

*"Run! Run! Flee for your lives! Climb into the hills! Women, take
your daughters, Men, take your sons, Run! Run!!"*

The shoreline water

slowly

     sank

the little combers

       stopped

the entire sea

          receded

yielding up the entire bay's inshore sands

   to light and sun

    then receded yet lower

      to the now-glistening far distant rocks

       where she, the most fearless of us all,

        went snorkeling

         saying it was the

          best in the area

     and there

in that bowl of those rocks

the distant wave first

   rose

    an ominous

     greasy

      ugly

       giant

        roaring under

         the sea's skin

now a rolling rise

high already

far distant two miles out

a mountain wall of water

thundering toward the beach

faster than any human

even athletic her

could

run,

even fleet Mercury with wings on his feet,
but even a god couldn't flee
this ungodly
colossus
of ocean power rising.

The shore dwellers
fleeing to the hills behind the village
atop which the Buddhist *vihara*
heaped itself
brick upon brick
into a solid dome painted white,
ran as fast as they could
mothers
fathers
running, running,
sons
daughters
screaming, screaming,
the doomed elderly hobbling behind,
the dogs frantically following in wailing wonder
at what all this meant,
all of them running, running
but still too slow,
too late.

The wave crested, leaped all over itself,
thundered onto the beach an unimaginably crushing weight
yet she
was still running
screaming
trailing the yellow and red behind
until she

vanished.

Vanished.

Justlikethat.

I could only hope
the crush of the wave was so massive
it broke her life
before she could suffer
the horrible panic and blackness
at the end of being without air
and the death agony begins.

The compassionate being in the brick *vihara*
is a useful trust
when life is cheap.
Nothing of her was ever found.
The village so many centuries old,
and all but a few of its people,
were never seen again.

Those wise in the way of the sea
know that by defying it
despite knowing its power,
the sea always wins
and does not win mercifully.

We no want you no-clothes lipstick type women
come our village, *lah!*
We village,
you big-city *lepak* layabout women,
not village, *lah!*

Our lives good,
men work, *waghhhh*, hard they work,
women cook, sweep,
children happy, *waghhhh*.
We no want daughters see
make-up type magzines you bring.
We this land, not you, *heinh!*
You no-clothes women
say you new-time we old-time,
Aneeeyyy!
We no want new-time,
Aneeeyyy.
We no backtalk men like you,
Aneeeyyy.
No want daughters go city school,
no come back.
Aneeeyyy!
Want village boys marry village girls,
no marry city girls.
They do, *lah*, what then?
Village go *ssst-ssst*,
dry up like chapati too hot.
You *Aneeeyyy sila*, our way of things, *lah!*
Timepast say all things given
we must do,
we not do, bad happen.
Then what?
Rice farmer use stone try stop leak
in *bisokotuwa* water sluice-gate,
water go over *bemma* paddy top,
whole paddy *waghhhh!* wash to sea.
Better lose little water than whole paddy.

Women got three faces.
First woman wear mask, no see other mask.
Second woman wear mask, evileye other mask.

Third woman got man,
man bring food.
Got kids,
girls women-work, boys man-work.
Got house, keep clean,
cook, eat, have babies, go temple,
no need mask.
You come, teach paper-book write.
Time-out-of-mind we sand-book write.
Finger draw in sand,
house picture fix house
cart picture
fix cart
temple picture
build temple.
Longtime
we know
right mix
water, cement
for when *vessa*
rain-time come.
You know this?
No.
You care this?
No.
You ask us?
No.
You come *lepak* layabout talk-telling us do your way?
Yes.
Waghhhh!
You second woman-mask type woman.
Waghhhh!

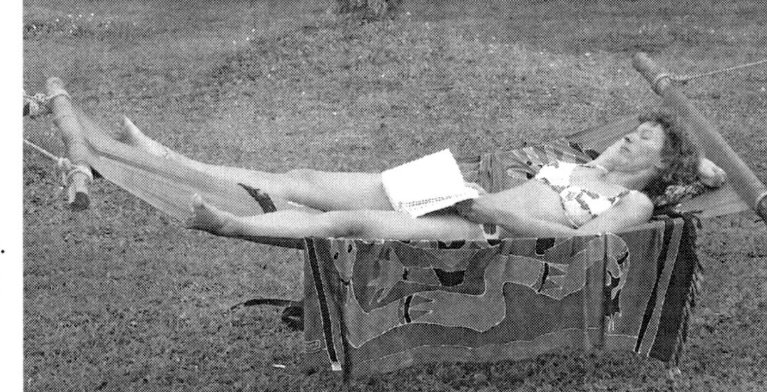

Enthralled by Winds of Loneliness

Drifts of resonance
cross separatrix connections
to *arjunadyhana* resting places
where we wish we could lie.
But to survive must after must
to feast of fruition,
survive the toil of tranquillity
that is the *jamu* garment
of ivory *flabellum,*
kahapana coins of copper,
leaf and flower of *malati*
tamali
navamalika
bimbijalaka
campala
asoka, tilaka, patali
nipa, jambu, kadamba,
earthsung gems offered to our eyes
amid *gamelan* accompaniments
to old Javanese languages of demeanor,
spoken in the elevated rungs
of neither fully wrong nor fully right—
wrong thing said right is right,
right thing said wrong is wrong.
So stings the brush of Lady Sei Shonagon
of *saluang* music in *Minangkabau* nightfalls,
the black-haired, scarlet-eyed, manqué concubines
man-trolling the malls,
the patterns of their deceits
following the patterns of their garments:
scallop shells and they're fish,
strung flowers and they're gardens,

clouds and they're sky damsels,
wave forms and they're the sea of fecundity.

Androgynous warp
achieves local vision
of wefted *ikat* bleed
with which you wear not what you are
but what you suppose.
Honshu melmac on linoleum tables,
Sunda lavender and Kelamantan pink,
Kra drabbles of karst and ochre,
red, too, and yellow and brown,
all under a bowl of wildfire sky,
Chinese ink,
Nadu Bharatya Natam,
Kufic letters as angulate as the fervor they inspire,
local villages of crawling crabs,
crocodiles and phoenix,
makara and *naga* and flail-tail dragons.

Gods give meaning to us,
we'd never find it in each other.
Not in our words said which really aren't meant,
nor words meant which really aren't said,
but in a visit to the market stalls
to hear the chaffer of the vendors,
or down by the docks
listening to the drunken boatmen sing.

The untranslated terms above—in Sinhala, Hindi, and Bahasa
Indonesia—do have meanings. It's irrelevant what those meanings are.
Simply enjoy lyricism in tongues that have no cognates in Western
languages. They're more language souls than language sounds.

Lusoga woman in Uganda

I, Woman

Into land smoothed
by the mattocks of a thousand suns,
I, woman,
cast into the harrowed gouges our numberless seeds,
entreating for another year Earth's tender *ubuntu* *
of giving to us all it has.
Time-out-of-mind memory whispers
from we know not when
that one day the sea shall rise and the wind shall shriek,
the withering bamboo shall cry to the skies for rain
but the rain brings only more heat
until the birds die on the wing
the animals bend to their knees
life falls into a broken heap
and only the magpies and crows
know the meaning of sustenance,
unaware how soon their time will come too.
The air-groomed rust of bridges and girders
thins until it breaks;
the mountaintops of grand plans fall
bolt by bolt into deafening roar,
perhaps never again seen,
perhaps to be shaped again one day
by a hand into a tool.
Ten thousand years of metropolis
vanish in hunger and moaning
without reflecting on the abyss made of mind
that triumphed over the fall of nature
but could not triumph over itself.

* * *

---

* A Xhosa word for selflessly giving whatever one
  possesses to aid another in greater need.

I awaken before dawn,
listen to the birds awaken with me,
carry two large pots with narrow necks
to the well. Or the spigot. Or the stream. Or the river.
I take a stick for the snakes, the rats, the crocodiles.
When full the pots weigh my arms till my shoulders almost break.
I arrange the three cooking stones on the ground,
place twigs, sticks, broken-off coconut fronds beneath,
light them, put on a basin and fill it with water.
While it heats I sweep the grounds before our mud and daub house,
place rice or millet or barley in a hollowed-out palm stump
pick up the handle of the pounding pole
crush the grains *thump-thump-thump*
then put them into the now boiling water,
add yams, cassava, manioc, green plantain.
The children awaken; they come begging for food.
I give them sweet sticky-grain cakes I made last night
of cooked rice, millet, barley,
sweetened with sugar-cane water squeezed
under my stone seed-husking roller,
or honey if the children have been lucky enough
to spot a hive far up in the trees.
My husband awakens. He wants his food before the children,
says he will go hunting, but I know better.
For him "hunting" is finding his friends
at the dram shop under the only trees in the village
where they will liquor away the day
boasting of sport teams, football stars, politics,
and bicker over the music they play
on the cassette player they bought with money
stealthed from my savings purse I so carefully hid.
I feed him so he will go away
and I can attend to the children.
The eldest boy's trousers are worn out at the knees
and I must sew patches snipped from older pants he outgrew—
and note that I do not call him "my" boy;

he is his father's boy and will furrow his father's path.
Then I make the children's breakfast.
The boys chase other village boys with sticks
as I sing stories to the girls,
pretty tales from no village I know,
where men behave better than our men,
but women are just as we are.
I put schoolbooks in the bags that hang from their shoulders
and off they go, three miles to the school, three miles back,
boys throwing rocks and clods of dirt,
girls emulating the chirps of the birds.

After they leave, all the laundry goes into a plastic tub
along with a little packet of Rinso;
I walk to the place of the washing rock near the water spout
where we women pound the sudsy clothes on the rock,
roll them up, squish out the soap, rinse, squish again,
and roll them into tubes to take home in the bucket,
and spread on the ground to dry.

I fold them and put them bundle by bundle
into the storage baskets under each of our hammock beds.
After all this I feed myself a little,
then assemble with the other women
under the tamarind tree.

The sun is nearly overhead now;
it is time to fetch sticks.
Each day it is harder to find fire wood.
After the men with guns came and cut down the forest
we had no more wind-broken branches to cook with.
We had to strip the brush more and more of its branches,
first the topmost twigs
then the stems
until the inevitable and unwanted happened.
We began to meet women from other villages,
who were fierce to us,
shouting we were taking their wood.
We could be fierce, too,
but that would not find new wood.
The bundles we carried back each day on our heads
grew smaller and smaller, the twigs fewer and fewer,
and none of us knew what to do.
But then it would come time to prepare the evening meal
and we would pound more grain, cook it, find greens if we could,
for soon our men would demand their dinner,
followed by the children slightly less insistent
but at least polite.
The girls would fetch water to wash the cooking pot
while the boys played football with their fathers,
and we would forget
about the search for wood,
as we had forgotten it so many times before.

One day a foreign white woman came to address us.
She spoke to another woman
who spoke our language but not like we did in the village.

Pre-Dravidian aboriginal children, above Devikolam,
Cardamom Hills, Kerala, India

She said she could help us change our lives,
showing us how to raise more food
with loans of small amounts of money
made by banks from far far away,
and with this we could clear ground and prepare the soil,
and buy seeds and shoots.
She said if we planted the right seeds
in a few years they would provide enough dry stalks and brush

for all our cookfires
and never have to leave home.
She said other things, too,
so wondrous we didn't know their meanings—
cellphones, new seeds we did not know,
sewing little dolls of our children for export.
We muttered to one another
this was not the world we knew
and did not want.
The woman said our men treated us like slaves.
We were very angry with her for that.
We said we were not slaves,
we were more free than this foreign woman come to our village,
for she had no family, no children, no home of her own,
while we guarded our village traditions,
knew the meanings of all the names of our gods,
in the trees, the water, the sky, and the songs of the birds,
the night sky, the moon, the stars moving to and fro across the sky
but always coming back to greet us and live with us.
And the sun god how so like us,
chasing away the demons of the dark
disguised as jackals or hyenas,
or night birds invisible in their flights
looking for open doors to enter
to snatch our children away never again to be seen.
How *dare* this woman, who knew none of these things,
tell us we lived in bondage and she could free us?
Did her fine words help her own women give birth as we helped ours,
comfort the children if the mother died,
and then adopt those children among us as we do?
What city woman would ever do such a thing?
Had she simply offered us the small loans
to grow more food
we might have been content.
But when she began to talk of our men
she showed how little she knew of our secret power.

Yes, we women may work hard,
but in return we control
everything that befalls our village.
Yes, we were given to a man
at an early age as a child bride,
had our pleasure parts cut away
so we would not lust,
and, if we survived,
bore our first child
shortly after our first blood.
But when we gave birth
other women were with us,
and what woman does not yearn
for others around her?
And who but we would grieve the children lost during birth?
And the five in ten who did not live to their second year?
We may not be loved by our men,
but we are loved by our children;
loved by the land, loved by the grace of food and sky and cloud,
the bliss of rain which gives green to the growing season.
We are loved by our gods, our shrines,
our guardian spirits that live in the stones of our cookfires.
We alone prepare for and celebrate the harvest feasts,
the festivals of the sun's return from the chill time of winter,
and its granting us respite in October
from summer's sear of heat overhead.
We alone know the mysteries and the rituals that guard the village.
We alone gather in the depths of night
to wail and howl away the devil-animals that lurk invisibly
at night when everyone sleeps.
Yes, the men might rule with the sun by day,
but we rule with the moon by night.
Did this woman not realize nothing happens in our village
without our spiritual seal?
It is true that a man's work is forced onto us in the day,
but once twilight has fallen

we give them back that work in nightmares,
and make sure of those they have plenty.
Men make history because they alone write it.
We make myth because we alone live it.

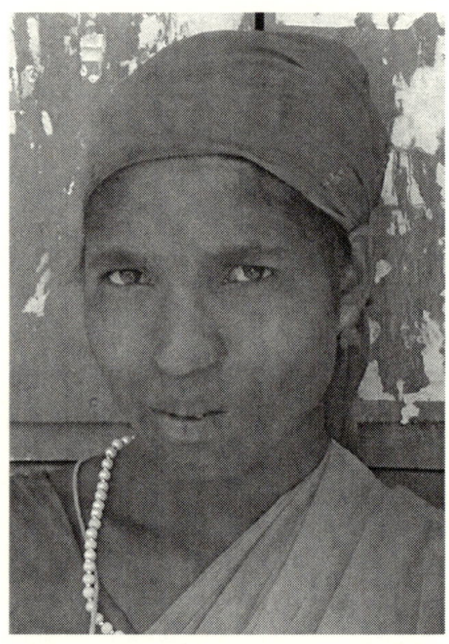

The men can vanquish all the other men they desire
but only we will win hearts.
When men think, their thought is good only for a day.
When women think, our thoughts make the future.
When men fight to rule the world
they end up ruling the ruins they make of it.
We women choose to rule over nothing,
so we may preserve our way of life.
When men fight to vanquish, the slightest mistake kills them.
When women fight to survive, the whole village survives.
If the task of men is to be important,
women's task is to be wise.
We make ours a good village, a great land, and a grand tribe,
for we give birth to the life and flesh of these.
The land cannot afford to lose us;
if it does, it loses our knowledge

that the land and the people are one.
Take away our gods and shrines, as the Christians did,
and we will bring them right back
disguising our gods behind the names of Christian saints.

A world without women would soon empty of people;
the loss of the wisdom we impart to children
would turn the fragile balance of all things
into a clockwork tinkle sounding the last hours of the earth.

The only good to come of a world without women
is that the forests would grow back.

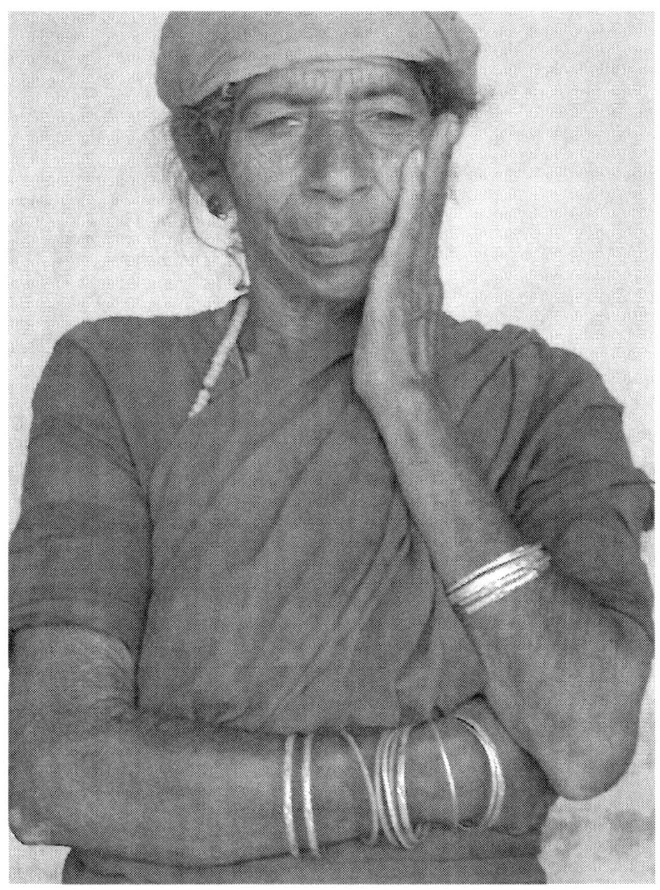

Dawn Train to Darjeeling

Day's
dusky rose hazes
loom tree colors like dawn-bright tulips.
Night's purple-greens hue into pastels of dawn
that seem more than exist.
High cirrus whipsilvers the sky.
Tropical bleach of heat and haze
begins even now, before the sun.
Clay roofs redden to blunt-edged blocks,
walls of white
windows of black.
A woman in a muumuu-like *kebaya*
wears tangerine scarves
on her way to the well,
hair pulled into a tight bun decorated with old Chinese coins
with a square hole in the middle.
A reclusive root yielded up its treasured rose-yellow
to the dyer who tinted her blouse,
and teased her skirt's fathomless purple
out of a boiling vat of crushed mangosteen skins.
Flaxen eyes,
hair like grass combed everywhichway by wind,
feet dusted the sandy tan of the soil beneath,
which in times long past was a beach.

Paddy country, this—
threshing pads,
clusters of white antheriums in a mosquitoey copse,
phalanxed harvest stems
concealing scorpions within.
Palm leaves green in the rising heat of suntassel sky
amid humid-day sweeps of casuarina

where thick grasses
rim the concrete pad of the village well.
Black blotches mark where paddy husk is burned
turning the fieldscape into tatters of green
blotted with smudges that inspired
the village's traditional textile weave of lore.

Morning haze clears,
day haze begins.
Colors thicken into their thing-given names—
earth, brick, orange, mango, aubergine, maroon,
coffee, tea, manioc, banana.
Metallic glints off spun alumium water jugs
carried on the canted lean of hips
seen on erotic statues of Khajuraho.
Once time takes hold
it gives long after its origins—
in politics, in religion, in the music and art
of a girl swaying her hips on her way home from the well.
A woman stoops at a fire.
Kids on bikes blur down a road, white shirts, blue pants.
Clotheslines limp their weight-sagged hues

of brown, red, orange, yellow, green.
Blossoms of bougainvillea
fountain down a wall.
The forlorn remains of a kite flutter in a tree.
Gravestones mildew away
was by was and did by did
till all that's remembered
is that stones in the bamboo grove
hide cobras.
Wispy leafless thistles, fences of crisscrossed sticks,
a lurching road navigates some paddies.
A woman with thick folds of cloth
wrapped around her knees
carries a basket of laundry to the village wash rocks
in the stream beyond a grove of teaks.

Lone watch huts dot vast gulfs of weedy paddy
where family elders shout at marauding elephants
that every year paddy owners
entreaty the government to shoot or take away.
Hills hue out of the heat
in scraps of silhouette.
Footfall geometries lace across soil,
between hand-smoothed mud walls,
arcades of fence line, tin roof, tree.
Men sit on a grave mound
prodding their fighting cocks.
Faces of a thousand browns
palette every ancient village.
Across a stream a mother and a boy
wind their way up a path.

The hills rise,
paddies become sloped, sculpted, abutted,
less meandered, more proprietal,
reflecting the jealousies of landowners on hills.
River to rivulet,
ridge to rim,
flat to meander,
rows of seedlings merge as they green;
first into paddy,
then staircases of paddy,
then terraces,
then hills,
then ridges
then region
then nation
then history
then culture
then in a direct line to the god
at the summit of everything,
The Five Treasures of Snows,
Kangchenjunga.

Musical Chairs

In a tiny ten-table cafe
in a tiny outdoors plaza
under a waxing Virgo moon,
zephyrs of evening
rose to end the day's heat.
Two men clattered through a hot backgammon match
with furious hurls of dice.
A tot of a girl two tables away
burbled the cafe-thing-names
she was learning on Mommy's lap.
A guitar and an oud duetted,
fingers like nightingales
among the slithery sounds of a shaken tambourine
and teaspoons on a tin can.
They sang a quavering Cretan love song
in voices like a sobbing mouse.
The music was like porcelain
everything in miniature and perfectly shaped.
Lamplit faces a liquor of the eyelids' languors.
The balcony above was decorated with painted gourds
like Christmas ornaments on a tendriled vine.
Cruets of vinegar and oil awaited the first salad.
Fresh-picked wildflowers,
a little lamp with amber-colored oil,
potted ficuses and oleanders between the tables,
slate stone pavings.
The four young musicians' voices
and angst-laden instruments
echoed off the chasmy stone walls
and Venetian-era iron balconies
of bygone-glory palaces.
A little girl twirled a flower under her nose.
The musicians had strong vigorous beards
and strong vigorous hands.

They gestured
with their fingers
the same way they sang with their instruments,
tunes of sliding harmonies and scales,
halts and slithers and major chords dwindling to minors.
One with a voice like the dying gasp of a sheet-metal shop
sang lustily of life behind the thick-walled windows
of his second-floor apartment with flower pots in the balconies.
So intent on their music were they,
the posh plucks that gave their oud its mournful air,
they were surprised
when a man softly applauded
and his companion in her garments of teal upon blue
presented them from the vase on their table
a single yellow rose.

Diwali lamp, Kateragama Kovil, Kandy, Sri Lanka

And Then the Lighting of the Lamps

Diwali comes in mid-October.
It's a homey Hindu festival
that celebrates family bonds with a day of gift-giving,
luxuriously delicious sweets,
visits to relatives,
calls upon doddering grandpas and aunties who never married
great uncles who smoke florid cigars,
young couples in modest residences already copious with kids.
The name Diwali is Hindi for "Festival of the Lights"
and it is around the household "lamp"—
a polished brass pedestal
with a petal-shaped ewer atop that holds six wicks—
that the Diwali festival takes place.
A saying goes, "A house without a lamp is a house without a home."
The lamp signifies the Light of Love reigniting the love
the household's couple had when they lit a similar lamp at the *kovil* (temple)
the day they were wed.

Diwali begins at sunset,
with a vast preparation for a family feast.
By the hour of tangerine-colored clouds,
the cooks are already scrubbing carrots and rinsing lentils.
As the sky paintbrushes its way down
through mixed shades of gray to twilight's
horizon-to-horizon arc of purple,
flowering trees first lose their luster,
then their color,
finally their shapes.
Cookfires flicker.
The *kampung* (village's) contingent of young girls chat

as they carry water pots to the village well,
returning with one canted on a hip, the other balanced on their heads.
Boys split firewood,
clusters of friends discuss the day's events in the middle of the road,
snakes wriggle their way to their bowers,
motorbikes jammed with whole families rasp by,
two-wheel tractors *pchink-pchink* along the roads
towing carts jammed to the gunnels with people
on their way to the lamp-lighting places.
These same *kampung* bus systems
serve moviegoers, black hair streaming in the wind,
as they chatter their way
to tin-roofed tin-walled village movie houses

with names like The Excelsior,
which feature twin bills comprising one
saccharine musical romance
and one American shoot-'em-up
with the bloodletting in slow motion
and subtitles that have people
laughing in the oddest places
as dying crooks go out in a hail of one-liners.
Entrance fees are one *ringgit* in the front row
where the impecunious sit Buddha-style staring almost straight up
to ten *ringgit* in the "Dress Circle,"
a row of chairs lined up on a riser in the rear.
No popcorn in this palace,
just peanuts still in their shells,
paper cones of chickpeas that taste like fermented wallpaper paste,
and melting ice cream crunchy with sugar crystals.
By the end of the show the floor is littered
with banana peels, mangosteen husks, and mango seeds.

Diwali takes place on the night of the full moon.
People walk from house to house to light the Diwali lamps inside.
They go in, light one of the wicks, pay respects,
nibble a sweet, go on to the next house.
In the now fully darkened evening an old man,

ghost in the low light,
hung flickering lamps like Christmas-tree ornaments
from the town square's low trees.
He wore a single yellow thread around his wrist
that marked him as a widower,
replaced each morning by the brahmin at his *kovil*.
One by one he brought out the lamps.
They flickered faint shades of yellow and rose
through their crinkled paper,
the candle held upright in the center
in a congealed puddle of its own wax.
A thin wire looped the lamp over the tree branches.
He wore a knee-length sarong and a T-shirt,
skin like twisted canvas,
muscles taut as stretched hawser.
He hung the lamps not for himself
but for his granddaughters who lived there.
He made the lamps;
the granddaughters supplied the candles.

Temple brahmin,
Munneswaram, Kovil,
Sri Lanka

The flames of the Agni of long ago
were mellow in him now,
just as they were in the time-out-of-mind past generations
that lit the same flickering lamps,
for the immense tremor of their tribe of Hindu,
for noble-headed Brahma, bull of the universe,
for Indra who gave India its name,
for Agni, the voice of the gods in the campfire and lamp,
and for the old man who himself became Agni
just by lighting the lamps.
Guests came, resplendent in saris and sarongs,
there was laughter, solemnity, soda pop, sweets,
babies spit up,
people laughed.
Then the lamps were all lighted
and only the night birds remained
to say when they guttered, sizzled, then flamed out.

.

Scribbled in Hong Kong Cafes

You spot the best Hong Kong working-quarter cafes
by their eloquence of drab:
fake mahogany-grain tables
on spindly aluminum-tube legs,
orange-red plastic chairs,
zig-zag linoleum floor tiles,
flailing overhead fans,
fluorescent lights,
Tsingtao beer ads in shades of bile and brown,
rubbish bins lined with brown plastic sacks,
brooms and industrial floor cleaner
stacked next to tomatoes and spring onions,
mildewed coolers filled with fizzy drinks,
red plastic cups medusing white straws,
frayed, reeking table-wiping rags (never washed),
stamped aluminum ash trays anodized a ghastly green—
and filled with so many people
there's hardly an empty chair.
The coffee is so strong
one cup is all a grown person can handle.
That explains the sign,
"Milk in coffee fi' dollah extra."
All this virtually screams
that the food is fabulous here.

Designer restaurants with smart polished tables,
black vases filled with orchids,
hanging scrolls too lavish with gold,
silver creamers, round doors painted Feng Shui carmine—
all this adds up to package tour groups,
oily dishes, a *LOT* of MSG,
and bacilli you won't discover
till you're back on the tour bus
on your way to the Mainland.

Talking as we await our food
we toy absently with dinnerware
upon which everything will soon change
and nothing scrutable remain.
Does anyone ever rise
from the dinner table's pain and ignorance
a hero
having earned the throne and the maiden?
We will never truly know,
for as soon as the hero sits
at the head of the table
he turns into a tyrant—
all in the good name
of his subjects, of course.
If the hero in us has a thousand faces,
why do so many of them age into a banker's?

That sage recluding in the mountains,
we entreaty for truth,
did he really attain The Way?
Is there hope whence he ventured,
or lies it only in the mystical dreams
dwelling in our Cimmerias of wish?
Shen Tsung-Ch'ien depicted hope
as a universe made of vital breaths
from which a painting attains excellence;
each breath does not flow
but rather emanates from the brush,
as our ponderings emanate from our emptiness.
Shih-t'ao also knew:
emptiness is full
and fullness is empty.
Cheng Pan-Ch'ao could depict an entire rock
with a single movement of the brush.
When he died his last words
were, "Thus should we live,
as one stroke of the brush."

Heroism is thus neither prince nor grail
but one stroke of the brush.

No fashion designer
is fooled by what hides beneath our clothes,
but few designers
see beneath our skin.
Almost none seek beyond our eyes.
Yet that is where our hungry ghosts lurk.
To understand who will be satisfied
with the contentments of illusion
designers must be more of the wearer
than they are of themselves.
That is why, when they sketch,
they must become more your ghost
than their own.

I reminisce over the old days,
and yes, they were so prized.
But they were umulscind,
a thin layer of image
atop a durable substrate of character
that, when developed,
became life's long quest for integrity,
and, alas, one with so few mileposts.

A one-minute 360-degree panorama
seen from a chair
in an outdoor cafe
yields persimmon storefronts
indigo shutters
pumpkin facades.
Red paper lanterns stream gold tassels in the sun.
A middle-aged man wears skin-tight black pants,
white shirt, black shoes with white socks—
visitors from the Mainland
aren't all that hard to spot

amid Shisheido's lupus lipstick
and Microsoft's digital dementia.
Mottled oranges pyramid a pushcart.
Women of a certain age wear retro bobs;
women thirtyish *Elle*-ad soft curls;
while defiant young fashion-forwards go for frizz cuts
(though neither defiant nor forward
to the point of tattoos and piercings).
Self-important *ah peks*
in their self-appointed uniforms
of blue silk shirts with white silk ties,
as pretentious and regimented
as office peons everywhere.
Off-whites and beiges mark mall-honed women;
pearls on black linen mark fashion sophisticates
who know to understate even the quiet tones,
always tailor with fabrics cut on the bias,
and don't even *think* of any but matte gold.
Red/yellow/blue primary hues identify off-the-rack buyers;
cinnamon/ochre/umbers identify made-to-measures.
Apothecaries stress spotless marble floors,
walls paneled with honey-colored wood,
and exquisitely floral unguent jars
holding powdered rhinocerous horn
tiger spleens
bear paws
and walrus tusks.
Sarong party-girls hither-eye prospective dates
with loosely-tied hints of more than hither.
Mammiliform American tourists just off the tour bus
pendule like papayas from a tree.
Teenage boys freckled with pimples—
the computer-nerd's fashion statement to the world:
"Not enough sex and too much mayonnaise."
The lemur look in a girl's eyes
as she warily gauges the iron river approaching
the intersection she wants to cross.

Late-teen musclemen adopt body-aware T-shirts,
black pegged-cuff trousers,
and a falsely modest white belt
to make sure everyone knows
they've trained in more martial arts
than an entire army can use.
Schoolgirls wear uniforms of sailor blouses,
short blue skirts, and book-bags—
the costume that, after dark,

is the look hookers adopt
to lure middle-aged men who were oversexed
during their long-gone adolescence
when girls studiously ignored their existence.

It's always a bit wistful
when the minute is over.
Shall we do it again?

Logarithmic dances of galaxy and cyclone

Dances in the Cage of Time

He lives in the old part of town,
a nice quiet quarter
of antique shops, small parks,
windweathered doors filled with tired cats,
elm-lined streets named after heroes.
Whatever his old life was, it left him well.

Dance 1

Calls 'im The Old Perfesser, they duz.
No one really knows, but 'e talks like one.
He collects stuff. Lots of it.
Oh Lawdy Dear, LOTS of it.
Face is known in all the shops that's got
old junky stuff 'e calls ephemera
an' I calls trash.
Pictures of towns four hunnert years old,
all three issues of a mag'zine wot only printed three issues.
One look an' I c'd see why—
put me t'sleep in a minnit flat.
Faded pictures of people's relatives he din't know.
What's 'e see in people 'e never knew?
Postcards ya can't read they'z so old.
OK, I guess, but still junk,
if ya wants my word of it.
W'ldn't allow a bit of it in my place.
He's got friends they comes over,
talks about all this stuff,
sippin' sherry 'n eatin' chocolates.
Boring as hell, you want my 'pinion,
an' even if you don'.
Affable, tho', I gives 'im that.
Kid with a new toy when 'e gets a new piece 'o
—well— . . . junk,

I ain't 'bouts 'ta put no fine point on 't,
ain't no other word 'cept junk.
But o' course I wdn' wan' 'im to hear
any 'o that. 'E's too good a tenant.
Twenny-seven years, almost long as me.
Knows a bit 'o everything, he duz.
Always 'xclaimin', stuff like
walkin' with his back to the sun
to see the opened faces of the flowers.
Not fer me, I sez. When I goes someplace
I sets my sights on where I gotta gets to,
an' don' waste no time
peerin' at th' posies.
'T'other than that 'e's th' quiet type,
rises early, never bothers, no pets, pays on time.
Lissens to some longhair named Vivaldi
but all I heerd wuz zzz–zzz–zzz an' then some more zzz–zzz–zzz
till I hadda zzz–zzz–zzz outta there or I wuz gonna zzz–zzz–zzz scream,
an' from what my kids tells me, he wouldn'a wanna hear that.
Calls 'is place a house o' conversation pieces.
Well, I seed it meself.
Ain't sure if that's a word I'd use.
Wicker chairs
brass thingies,
funny old clothes hung up on a dummy
wot looked like the olden-times French king
after 'is head got chopped off.
Lotsa dust—
O Mother Mary pray my soul, *that's* fer sure.
Dumbest stuff me eyes ever crawled through.
Cabinets, old books, brass telescope, masks from Africa—
one time I made th' huge mistake
of askin' 'im where Africa was.
Couldn't get out of there for two whole hours.
Don' think 'e never stopp'd f'r a single breath.

Dance 2

In his room is a special window
painted to bathe the room in creamy light.
On its sill he brews a special drink
made of figs and oranges
steeping in honey and yeast.
It makes a mild refreshment,
perfect with tea at four.
He's been drinking it for ages
and says it's the secret of his health.
But then he veers from that with,
"Of course, when the subject of self comes up,
one must first endure the presence of caterpillars
in order to enjoy the presence of butterflies."

Dance 3

Then to the room above
comes a new tenant,
a woman of wild words,
scented garments,
astrology,
wildfire glances,
hours of dark sleeplessness.
She plays music full of rhythms
and speaks the nakedest words anyone ever heard.
Her eyes and her clothes
are purple and sheen,
and her lips sputter what lies at the core of her being,
a spume of curses spit into ideas
sweating into the late night.

Dance 4

I shudder'd all over, I looked at 'er place.
Smelled like a 'orehouse wot never changed perfume.

"'T's not a room, 't's a box full o' cracked glitter,"
sez I 'ta him one day,
"Mark my words: trust her no more
'n you'd trust the 'ips of 'n ol' whore."
Then ya know what he sez?
He sez, "Is it not better
to be free with a few words
than empty and in jail?"
Eyes popped out 'e said that, mine did.
Whose side'z 'e on, anyway?

Dance 5

Then one day, cerebral and without song,
she comes up to greet him.
He marvels at her truth to herself,
her smashing at the memories
time erases into walls.
She tells him of her teachers,
surrounded by mirrors scrawled with pat phrases.
"Sometimes it's that way," he consoles,
"when thinking of times past.
But while you're slicing at shadows,
the you hiding in your you
yearns to be flying.
What do you see
in the part of you that can dream?"
"I hate all dreams, they murmur over my thighs.
I want to jump off the arrow of time
before it hits and suddenly I'm you
and your chrondic eyes."
"You'll never get anywhere that way;
you have to create your own time
and set sail on that."
"From what I see as I look around here,

you put up your sails, all right,
but you never got out of dry dock.
The things in this room have horizoned your mind,
how can you live up here in all this dust
with no one that's real people?"
"Castles in the air
are easier to keep up
than ones on the ground."

Dance 6

But down in the old places
they begin to wonder where he's been.
The landlady lets slip a sly fact:
"'E's moved 'is desk nearer the window.
Said 'twas better to see the people in 'is old photos
but I seen his eyes
and they wuzn't lookin' there.
So I flat trumped 'is aces on 't.
"With keys of neglect," I sez,
"yer lockin' up yer days."
An' he says, "My days are a cup
that always lacked liquor."
An' I sez, "'Tis a child of dark wonder
what can so make you change yer truth,"
an' he sez,
"In a room full of conversation pieces,
with whom you can speak."

Dance 7

While upstairs in her noise shield,
she forgets him faster
than the moss
on the bricks of her old school.

Donkey saddle, France

Drawings and city views from Braun and Hogenberg, *Civitates Orbis Terrarum*, compiled starting 1572, and published 1617.

Paris, Place de la Bastille, 1539

The farmers who come to market in the evening
say, "Who sleeps with his animals at dusk
sells first in the morning."
   And they come.
   Toward twilight,
   dust-laden, tired,
   converging from the side paths and tracks,
   they come.
Riding sidesaddle on the backs of their oxen,
shuffling along leading their mules,
legs steady in their rhythms,
prodding along their animals
with the tassel-ends of long whips,
   into Paris's contours of
   cityscape and populace,
   they come.
Behind them,
astonishingly laden animals and carts,
almost invisible under their burdens
of kindling for fires,
pouches of dried fruit,
mounds of fodder for the animals,
baskets woven to pass
winter's long nights.

   Donkeys wheeze
   beneath sacks brimming with nuts,
   apples,
   wheat,
   greens from creeksides,
   barrels of back-shed wine.
Leather and hemp twines are taut to their breaking point.

They pay the entry impost,
move through the portals.

    The universities, archbishops, rectors, princes, garrets, garlic

        peelers, streets, castles, cathedrals, portals, roofs of Paris—
these sum to nothing.

    Paris means marketplace.

    It has stalls.

    That is enough.

They weave unerringly through the labyrinth of streets,
heading for the square with the tented arcade around the edge,
the Place de la Bastille.
     The light is now thinning.
     They hurry.
When they arrive at the familiar stalls,
the women make ringlets of stones
in which they kindle twig fires.

Children blow at the flames until the air froths with sparks.
     On go basins of water for soups,
     thin-hammered pans filled with quickbread doughs,
     scraps of meat on skewers,
     mugs to warm the wine,
     water for washing.

The men first unload the hay
to feed the animals.
While they are docile,

the men's sons hobble their legs to large stones on the ground,
then loosen the intricate knots that release their wares.
Enormous mushroom-shaped blankets
lose their shape as off come the baskets,
ristling to the ground with soft sounds of wickerwork.
Everything is arranged into a circle
to be covered for the night with rush mats and straw,
a lumpy but effective bed for the dogs.
A dozen chickens cackle together.
One pecks out at a passing ankle,
jutting its legs backward
to reveal that all of them are tied together
with a twine of briar runners.
The briar still bristles its thorn—
no harm to a chicken
but a sure deterrent for thieves.

As the animals
are unladen
the men stroke
their backs
and check their
halters for chafing.
Their work
then done,
they look for
familiar faces.
Wineskins begin
their gruff rounds
in swallows and belches.

The low-voiced speech of men
accustomed to hard labor
rumbles along with curses and guffaws.
They stay away from the inns and wineshops,
with their fast-talking men
with playing cards,

shell games,
tales of easy winnings too good to be true.
They all learned.

                    Once

                    was enough.

So mingling together
in the kind of talk they alone know,
amid the smells and unkemptnesses
of lives entwined to necessity,

they speak of harvests and weather and droughts and kings.
Silence comes over them
as a party of tax collectors
arrives on the other side of the square,
surrounded by armed guards
wearing white and blue fleur-de-lys,
each on his own horse.
(Horses! — How many unplowed fields
could be planted with the help of that strength!)
The tax men will dine with the market officials
and sleep at the inn.
The farmers will sleep on the ground
with their wives and children,
the cattle,

dogs,
chickens,
dried beans.

It is fitful slumber,
disturbed by the shifting animals and the cry of the watch.
A child's bleary eye marks the watch's passage:
half a dozen armed men
carrying flaming oil-soaked rags
guttering pale yellow light
from the end of long poles.

In the morning,
almost before the swallows
have begun their *skreeks*,
this is what they hear—

Local Pharmacy, Paris, 1539

And if you fail to be fixed,
may my ventpeg slip,
my stopper fail me,
my poop-pipe collapse,
and my fundament fall out!
Is there any man or woman among you
to say that it's contrary to law or faith,
against any reason,
not self-evident,
or opposed to Divine Writ?
No!
Far from it!
There's not a word in the Holy Book
that stands against it!
I ask you to look back on your days
and count the number of times you've had

farts with or without sound,

coughing spells,

sweating states,

sneezing attacks,

hiccups that

won't stop,

bad breath,

hemorrhages,

ague,

bad sleep,

bad dreams,

bad eliminations,

the rash,

attacks of tears,

paroxysms at any hour,

mucus from your nose,

hemorrhoids,

or spells of the wheeze!

If so, God's good merciful name be praised!

He hath turned your feet to me today!

For who among you

will say it cannot be true?

Ha-haaa!

May I drop dead on this very spot if a single word I say

is a freewilliger lie!

Made from a secret formula

by the mystic apothecaries of Galore,

it contains exotic dried roots,

fruits,

leaves,

berries,

gums,

seeds,

barks,

and juices.

There's not a wise-woman alive

who wouldn't churn it,

whirl it,

jumble it,

tumble it,

stroke it,

beat it,

bump it,

tweak it,

bang it,

shake it,

lift it,

clip it,

eye it,

smell it,

breathe it in,

look at it twice

and breathe it back out,

fondle it,

splash it,

whiff it,

stuff it,

swig it,

savor it,

sip it,

relish it,

enjoy it,

smack her lips at it,

belch twice,

and declare it

ambifanfrelucheLATEDly good

for oils and boils,

breaks and shakes,

quivers and shivers,

colds and molds,

Shaman baskets, Rissani, Morocco

sneezes and wheezes,

sweats that wet,

cases of bile,

and attacks of catarrh!

There isn't a piddle,

poop,

sob,

sneeze,

cough,

snore,

sweat,

hack,

bark,

mewl,

whoop,

snort,

snivel or snuff,

howl or yowl,

wiggle or waggle

that won't throw up its hands

and run for the rear door!

Sharp nose,

sunken eyes,

hollow temples,

cold ears,

tight forehead,

hurting gums,

wrinkled eyelids,

blue veins,

and frousoussulated teeth!

Gone, ladies and gentlemen,

*gone, GONE, GONE! **

---

* Assembled from individual roundelays recorded in *Les Cris de
 Paris*, a compilation of market-stall and hawker cries dating from
 the 1500s to the fall of the ancien régime in 1789.

Khori Tumed

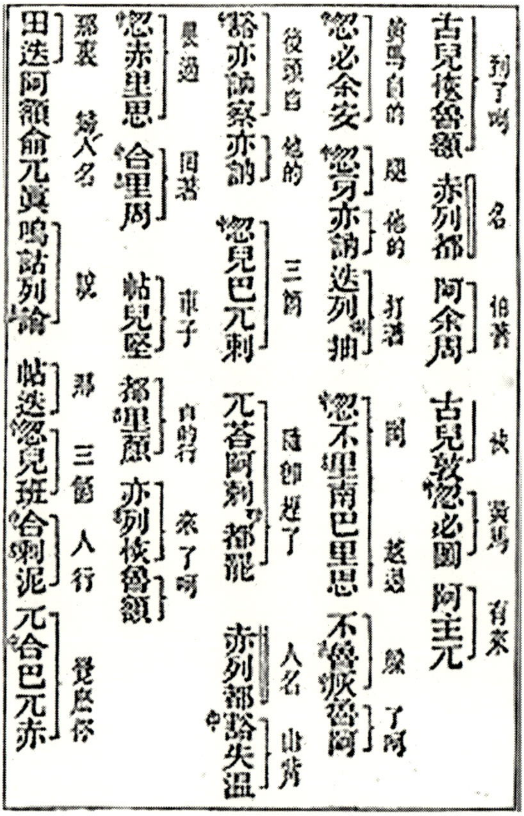

到了呵 名 伯著 衣 黄馬 有來
古兒伕魯額 赤列都 阿余罔 古兒敖惚必圖 阿主兀
黄馬自的 脚 他的 打着 剛 趕過 線 了呵
惚必余安 惚牙亦訥迭列抽 惚不里南巴里思 不魯灰魯阿
後頭自 他的 三箇 隨即 趕了 人名 山背
豁亦訥察亦訥 惚兒巴兀剌 兀荅阿剌都罷 赤列都豁失温
晨過 同著 車子 自的行 來了呵
惚赤里思 合里罔 帖兒堅 都里顏 亦列伕魯額
那裏 婦人名 說 那 三箇 人行 覺察得
田迭阿額侖兀真 鳴詁列論 帖迭惚兒班 合剌泥 兀合巴兀赤

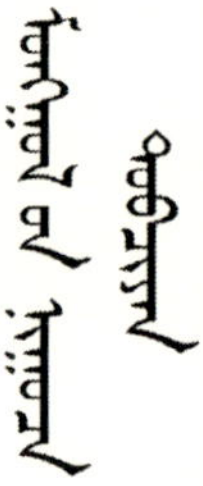

From the 1908 Chinese edition of the *Secret History of the Mongols*. The Mongolian text is in Chinese transcription, with a glossary following the large brackets to the right of each column. The vertical script to the left is the title *Secret History of the Mongols* in *Mongyul kele*, also known as *Khalkha*.

Mother of Swans

One day Khori Tumed saw nine swans
flying toward a nearby lake.
When the swans removed their feathered garments to bathe,
Khori beheld that they were beautiful women.
Thinking they were alone
the women splashed and played.
But while they were enjoying their play,
Khori stole one of the feathered garments.
When the women left the water
one swan was dismayed
that she could not find her garment.
Khori Tumed stepped from behind a tree
and insisted that she be his wife.
She had no choice but to consent.

They eventually produced eleven sons.
One day she asked Khori Tumed
to give her back the feathered garment
so she could again be a swan.
At first he refused, fearing she would immediately fly away.
But after repeated entreaties he finally relented
if she would assure him
she would not fly away.
She promised.
But when she put on her feathers
she was compelled by her swan woman within
to fly out the window and away.
Hearing his pleas for her to return,
she circled their home eleven times,
giving each of their sons a swan name as she did so.
Then she flew away to Swan Lake
and never returned.

Version II

Glittering Visitor of Night

During the lifetime of Dobun Mergen
his wife Alan Гoa had two sons,
Begünütei and Belgünütei.
After he died Alan Гoa did mot marry again.
In time, she bore three more sons,
Bukha Khatagi, Bukhatu-Salji, and Bodonchar Munkhag.
This naturally raised suspicions of the worst kind.
Her two oldest sons accused the three younger ones
of being fathered by an Uriankhai servant.
The younger ones felt slighted by this,
and soon enough there was talk of arms being used.
Hearing of these plots,
Alan Гoa summoned her five sons for a meal,
and gave them each one arrow,
and told them to break it.
They did so easily.
Then she made a bundle of five arrows
and asked them to break it.
None could do so.

Alan Гoa is a mythical figure from the *Secret History of the Mongols*, eleven generations after the Grey Wolf and the White Doe, and ten generations before Chinggis Khan. Her five sons are considered the ancestors of the various Mongol clans. "Г" is pronounced as if uttering "Q" or "Kh" while simultaneously clearing one's throat.

Alan Гоа told them that her three younger sons
derived from a glittering visitor
who came through the roof of her yurt each night
by crawling on the beams of the moon,
and left each morning
by crawling on the beams of the sun.
She told all her sons
that the three younger ones were children of heaven
and it was wrong to compare them with ordinary people.
She advised them that if each tried to go his own way,
they would be broken like the five single arrows.
But if they remained together like the bundle of five arrows,
nothing could harm them.

Drawings and city views from Braun and Hogenberg, *Civitates Orbis Terrarum.*

Kermis in the Year of the Plague

Down in the meadow a *loure*,
a countryman's bagpipe squalls
half-hidden in the mist-thinned distance.
November soundscapes between cobbles and roofs
prepare for winter.
Wash water and the contents of chamber pots
hit the street with a thick *swopp*.
Whispery sounds scurry from an old woman—
fastpatter sandalscuffs vanishing
into the giant dull thuds of an oxcart plod.
Masons' chisels clink at bricks;
a carpenter's adze gouges a new yoke for an ox.
Cleaning women whistle in their breath
bracing for the weight of their buckets.
Sausage sellers rearrange their bins
to the whiney accompanient of mongrels.
Chaos to the eye
but to the ear a midafternoon chord:
hay rustling
donkeys braying
coins slapped on barrel tops
haggles over eggs
horse wheezes
boy yells
bellows hiss
rapid footfalls on some mission of urgency
ruffles of bedding taken in from windows
dustcloth snapsclamations.
Milkmaids prod their cows with sticks and mutter *Hyoop*.

A ragpicker's broken-wheeled cart
clacks over the stones
as he rings his bell and sings his song.
A furious clatter comes from an official's wagon
as it careens to a halt;
the footman's steps gurgle in the mud
as he rushes to the door.
Two cackles and a cluck
signal precedence among three hens.

Tiny moments of euphony
break the monotonous cacohony
as small silences nap lightly on day's end.
Flies hover over broken fruit.
A woman cracks mustard seeds
with the back of a spoon.
Five bold bongs from the new town clock
are followed by a faint protest of four
from the neglected steeple down in the old bourg.
A man with a wooden leg
hesitates to cross a street,

then finally dares
clinging to his rustling basket of breads.
A slurry of bulrush sounds
blurs from a basket weaver on her way home.
Leaves rustling in a gutter
mark a cat closing in on a bird.
A chomp goes by
holding in its hand an apple.
Hair swept back and clinched by a pin,
a merchant's daughter dressed in black
brushes aside all the others
with a haughty swish of cape.
The smoking volcano of a newlywed's argument
seethes past on rising heat,
words spitting from the tight fissures of their lips.
A young butcher's apprentice
comes wine-sliding along,
and laughs uproariously as he loudly propositions
a heap of flaxen concubine hair.

and release us from our sins.
We all will sing
and we will RISE!

Then to the granary at the edge of the field
where the bagpiper still squalls
his brocaded tattoo.
His cheeks puff into a wooden tube
and under his arm he holds a pigskin
sewn tight to hold a lungful of air.
Two pipes come out
to loop over his shoulder
tassels on the end
with a foxtail between.
These pipes moan the tonic tones
around which his fingers
string the tune.
What he lacks in rhythm
he makes up for in imaginings,
fingers chasing out notes
thick as mosquitoes in midsummer.

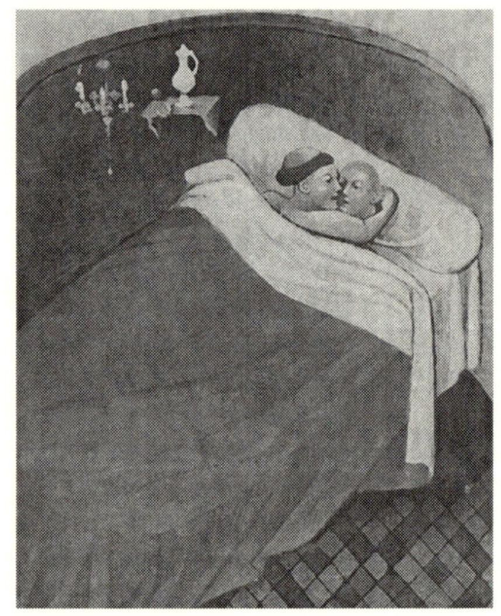

A chain dance forms
     serpentining colors and hands.
       Young girls begin first,
          practicing with each other
          to get the steps right,
          then flirting at the knots of boys,
          the bowlines of faces
          they hope to untie with their eyes.
A moon-faced flutist joins the piper with a nod.
     With a bob of his head he catches the pace
     wails high a soprano world
     faster than time in the night.
          Beneath him a tambourine
          clomps of wooden shoes
          slaps on bent knees.
The piper hurls out the first few notes of a catch
     the flutist goes still faster
     to garnish them with grace notes and trills.
          Then the embroidery thins
          their notes glide out onto a song.
     It's an old tune the entire *kermis* knows,
  smooth, so twined with glides
they all wish they were a snake
     and so they are:
          arms link and furl in the sly sex
          of the S-dance.

The girls' seriousness softens
from doing it right to doing it for fun
dancing each other into riotous melting colors.

A reedy *hautbois* joins the platform.
The mood of the dance changes
from curtseys to swung arms
spangle sounds from wristbells.
A kiss slides by halfway through a turn,
and a surprised face vanishes away
into the two-step beyond.
Bonnets fall and are snatched up in midbeat,
hair shakes loose in the tremble of the tune.
A proud potbelly launches into a reel,
turning a quick four-step
into a two-step glide
carried with such aplomb
it is almost like grace.

Another kiss is grabbed,
   this time held for a handful of beats.
A baby's chin is tickled as it sucks
on a soothing sack of mint tied in a cloth.
      A ball-shaped wad of wool
      stuffed with damp grass
      escapes from a circle of playing boys
      and rolls lumpily into the dance.
      A dozen feet field it
      and it goes spurting back out
      erupting grass as it flies.
Two old sots dressed up for the occasion
   with boots erupting grasses
   pants stuffed with leaves
   grotesqurifessé queue et les couilles
   with entwined nosegays.
      They kiss a toothless old woman,
      and with exaggerated bows
      lead her to the edge of the dance,
      holding her arms up in an imitation sarabande.
She remembers most of the old steps,
dancing at half the pace of the younger folk
but with the same eyes.

Now the dance breaks loose from the chain.
   Evereyone links elbows two by two
   weaving a complicated knot that ends in a circle.
      Bow to the right, curtsey to the left,
      then left foot out,
      into the pivot and then the twirl,
      ending face-out linked-arms in a circle.
But the bagpiper knows it's only eight beats
   and shakes out a bagful of trills.
      The dancers spin and link arms for the Grand Tour.
Wristbells flow into cuffs,
beltpurses and wineskins swash in an apron sea.

They swoop a hand-exchange over their heads
and are back to the original pairs.
A last sprinkle of grace notes
gives way to a wheeze.
The dancers bow and smile
in the sudden vast silence of the dance's end.
A wad of grass goes unfurling through the air,
strewing over two young lovers
chiding them for dancing too tight.

Fishing family, Semenanjung Minahassa, Sulawesi (Celebes)

Sails Unseen Across the Sulawesi Sea

I apprenticed my youth to a Cambodian bird-feather gleaner,
the clan that furnished the world
with the intense blue feathers
only royalty could wear.
Together we went a-dhowing the Sulawesi isles
sailing the riverine isles to Araby
and betweentides slept in Borneo too,
with the Melanau
the Dyaks
Budiah and Bidayuh
Iban
the people along the Saribas River
who called themselves *Kami Saribas*
"We Saribas"
for to them their river and they
were one in the same.
I was at the ancient healing ceremonies
of *berbayah* and *berayan*
sold *belum* get-well fetishes
to the Selukau people of Lundu and Sematan
stored my memories in Martaban jars
I bought from riverboat vendors of Mukah
who supplied the mangrove dwellers with goods.
I then bought from them *pua kumbu*
talisman carpets
from the women on the slopes of Santubong,
and traced the arabesques of Uzbeki pastels
on the masjid side of town.
Yes, yes, O yes that, and yes of much else, too.

I was there
river bathing with the Tedayan
feasting with the Orang Minik
laughing with the Bakong.
I chaffered with the Dalek of Bintulu and Miri,
danced with the Dayak at their *gawai* harvest festival
lived among the Bukar Sadongs in the Serian
among the Biatahs of Kuching
the Singgais of the Bau
the Jagoi
the Lara
the Kayan in the upper reaches of Apo Kayan
that soft, brown eel-kiss of a river so limpid its flow
where one can smell each color and hear every taste;
then ascended upland to Usun Apau above Kenyah
to where Sarawak becomes Kalimantan.
I am Kelabi, Penan, Lun Bawang.
Ferns grew from the boards of my weary docks,
the brownish gray of windweathered wood,
doorways filled with glim-eyed cats.
I was the art of the Orang Ulu with its eerily Kwakiutl feel
flat faces with wide features;
and too am I Kayan fetishware
demonically composited of wild boar ears and human eyes.
I am why the Melanau carved miniature coffins
into burial posts
door guardians
lobe ends of paddles
fishing amulets from bone and antler
and the most elaborate and fantastic part
of the *burung kenyatang*
the sacred hornbill
or more exactly
its highly imagistic false coxcomb
so strangely Aztec-like in features
that do not exist on the real bird,
and I wondered from which recess in our commonality

comes the impulse to fantasy
and is that recess mayhap where our troubles began?

Yes, me.
Bedazzled, begalleoned, bestrewer of dream deeds
from Mantai in Serendib to the Solomons I plied
kingfishers for blue
macaws for beak
orioles for yellow
parrots for everything else
(for when it comes to colors parrots don't miss a trick).
O yes, yes, O yes,
sun and soil, night and day,
quick life and quick death,
I saw those, too,
the tiny insect bite on a thumb
growing blue then black for no reason
and how the eyes gape in the end
screaming because the voice no longer can.
I was there, too, marrying multiply
not for why the tawdry may think
but because time in common is precious
and time alone is meaningless,
and because of four sons who would go to sea
in ten years time three widows would make.
My feathers bought salt
which I traded for pearls.
I planted cereals,
I burnished utensils,
coiled clay ropes into pottery
and into those pots coiled ropes,
for the coil is to me as commonplace
as the petrol pump hose is to you.
The ropes I then sold to sea gypsies
who passed the rainy season
in dwellings on stilts,
not that they should remain dry in the rains

but to keep the rats away
and therefore the snakes.
I wove *kajang* and *attap* mats for wall and floor,
hewed woods with sharp stones,
built megaliths and dolmens
for my spirit and nature gods.
In Kelbit I told the chiefs
that to inspire their subjects to revere their mortal remains
so they would be thought of as gods
(a notion they rather fancied)
they should take to embalming themselves
atop a hollowed tree
copper inside bronze and that inside iron
till they turned into the ages
that all may see.
Three thousand years past I left behind stone slabs
which for curious reasons the *farangi* termed "artifacts"—
now please, please, dear scholars,
those are immortal remains
you temporize with that name.
If I used the word "megalith"
would it open a different window on the matter?
"Mega" may strike a certain resonance in you,
but it strikes dissonance in me.
I deem myself not grand, nor am I great,
I am but my people
and we are not a me,
we are a We.
I use "I" because I am obliged to write it in your tongue
even though I know that while you might see my point
you will never grasp its meaning.
I whose thriving traces back three thousand years
of docking cargoes
hewing iron adzes
kilning pots large and small
with twilight-blue lapis,
seafoam-green malachite,

celadon,
jade.
I, who have brought to my world
ground-glass beads
fragrant sandalwood
silkwood (and not for nothing is it so named)
nests made by bespittling sparrows
animal horn
camphor
purpura
orchil—
all this, all,
from the I who is not an I but a We,
and mind the upper case, please.

You think this is academic, arcane, tribal, remote,
don't you, my friend,
the railings of a mind past its prime.
Ahhh, but just wait,
my unfurling sails sing
of your long slide into dwindledown time
and you'd better listen why.
You have waged a war that defeated yourself
and made enemies of the friends you once had,
and you are about to hear from me of our revenge.

The refined classes from Santubong to Rome
relied upon my sliver-thin hull
to ply the Silk Sea,
no less glorious a tradeway
than the thousand-camel caravans
bedusting the Silk Road.
From Pegu in Burma
from Aceh and Mataram
Melaka in Malaysia
Cochin-China to the Kochi of the moormen
Ternate in remotest Palawan,

all these but a gurgle
beneath the woven reed sails of my lateen
Out, yes, yes, O yes,
out to as distant as Maguindanao
the Isles of the Thieves.
And when on the other side of the silver sun,
those rustics the pirates of Sumatra
fancied themselves important enough to ally
with the bumptious new state of Kediri,
I threw out the King of Kediri
to much cheering from the crowds
as he rose sixteen cubits into the air
and vanished into a black cloud that rained gold glitter.
I replaced him with a tribesman of the Singhasari,
of whom soon I also found wanting,
so replaced him with a Majapahit,
and soon yet again in their own due time,
I molded all these bits of trade and tribe into Srivijaya.
Which I count as rather a bauble to my credit,
for my *Ramayana* is still retold in its every boisterous nuance
with leather puppets acting the great drama
behind sheets strung on a rope from two limbs
lit from the rear with fire lamps,
via which village theater prospered
until electricity brought television
and doomed my time, my children, my history, and me.
"My" *Ramayana?* you demand with raised brow.
Yes,
"My."
I didn't write it, I *am* it,
and if you follow its ancient plot in full
you will realize how subtle I am
how intricate my thoughts
how quietly I lurk despite enormous passages of time,
by which the culturally astute among you
will readily foresee my rise

atop the dust crumbling off the edges
of your supremacy.

But as this recital is belaboring your ears excessively as it is
let us move beyond my Jambudipa days
save to say that they sure were fun
(frightful lot of idols, though).
My *Berjaya Melaka* endhowed Siam to the Moluccas,
wiped out the pirate nests of Pontiniak, Brunei, Bandjarmasin,
turned them into respectable trading ports,
with temples, docks, and a stuffily prosperous merchant class
—and if you object to bourgeois values,
remember that citizenries don't start wars
like those cowardly curs the politicians.
I spun tops into the game of *main gasing,*
flew kites into the aerial combats of *wau bulan,*
took them to regions that adopted them as pastimes,
and visited on the way the feast tables of India,
China, Khmer, Kutch,
Sindh,
the better to savor the tasties when back in my House of Malaya.
I gave everyone *tuak* rice wine and taught them to dance.
And urban source code,
I gave that, too,
but it took two thousand years
to be made manifest in the Petronas Pair of Kuala Lumpur.

A bit melodramatic, you say?
Be forewarned: I am about to lead you into your cultural future,
where you will be obliged to live under me,
as I was once obliged to live under you.
You have trampled my family album
For nigh six hundred years;
it is now my time to tread upon yours.
You think of your culture Occidental
as one

good
true
beautiful.
Well, I do not.
I take you to be mirror-loving fools
whose sun is about to set
as mine is about to rise.
Why?
Because you dismissed me without a thought.
You saw surfaces when I am depths.
You extracted and shipped all my minerals
till they groaned the strakes of your hulls,
then sent back overpriced gadgets in exchange.
I have given you three thousand years of unbroken past
and quarterly reports is all you offer in return.
Now, my friend, it is your time to savor
the bitter gall I have tasted for centuries:

I know the chivalries in your *Heimskringgla,*
do you know the chivalry of my *Hang Tuah* and *Hang Jebat?*
I know how your Villon laughed away the choking noose;
do you know how my Töng Chih laughed away
the boiling cauldron in the court of Sun Ch'an?
I know the shedding of worldly *nostalgies*
in your poems of Hèloise;
do you know the verses in which my Ho Nansorhon
shed too her tears?
I know your Magna Carta and Constitution;
do you know my *Upanishads,* my *Sejara Malayu,*
my *Vamsas* of ancient Asian pale?
I know your Gilbert and George and your Tamara de Lempika;
do you know my butterball infants painted on glass in Tanjore?
I know your Pied Piper;
do you know my *lagi tutu lagi incit?*
To you your erudition is amazing.
You know all about yourself

and hesitate not to say so,
yet you have not a clue of any I have just said
and care even less.
You who limn the night away
preening before your codependency mirrors
are soon to discover I have my enablers too . . .

> *In the Spring of the year Uryu*
> *when I was young and in my morning*
> *I climbed a mountain of beads and jade rising from the sea.*
> *Peak upon peak of white above blue sparkled and dazzled*
> *till I was able to see with the eyes I wore as a child.*
> *Rainbows shrouded the peaks*
> *and the springs welled up with red gems.*
> *Between the rocks I followed a languoring cloudward stream;*
> *strange plants and exotic flowers everywhere,*
> *leaves wearing jackets of scarlet and great green hats;*
> *phoenix, cranes, peacocks, kingfishers sprang onto the path*
> *urging me upward withal their sweet sounds.*
> *When I reached the summit*
> *the great seas of the four directions*
> *joined me to the sky and all became emerald.*
> *The sun rose red and bathed me in wind,*
> *the pool at the summit was deep and clear,*
> *heart-of-lotus raindrops shone in my eyes.*
> *A voice said, "This is Mount Kwangsang*
> *the best on all continents.*
> *You must be one of the Immortals*
> *or you would not find your way here.*
> *Please write of us in verse and take away with you*
> *our Spring and Autumn Annals,*
> *and tell the world you saw shimmering in the sky*
> *the most distant land*
> *of Noni Tawangsari,*
> *on the other side of the sky."*

Did your blessed Petrarch so lyre upon descending Ventoux?

Lagi tutu, lagi incit, my friend:
Every child is everyone's child.
I am ageless, subtle, patient,
and now ruddering toward my nearing time.
What use have I for your pointless erudition?
It will all wither in times to come.

And now
Grand Emperor of the Occident
I finally demand of you:
Petrarch, Petrarch,
where were you
when my forebears
plied the Sulawesi Sea
and I went a-sailing
to *Noni Tawangsari?*
Why do you assume I must learn so much of your culture
while you have no need to take note of mine?
Does it not give you pause that I know far more
of the jokes lurking in this recitation
than you know of we *Kami Sulawesi?*
That I can make japes at your expense
and you scent not the faintest trace
of the burnt sugar in my humor?
In the above toccata to my heritage
and fugue upon your own
did you know a single name
or place of which I spoke?

O fool! For the past six hundred years
I have been carving my future
upon those megaliths of my origins
while you, of my dimensions or numbers
or consequences or intentions or patience,
know nothing.
Your days are done of doing the telling and not the asking.
Ride high, my friend, upon your neigh of insolence
and enjoy the view from your peak of patriciate.
My seabed is rising
while you kick aside the stones which made yours
and in the earth-ringing rage of when I shear
you will not even then have realized

C'est moi, vos deluge.

Copies of this book may be purchased
from your local bookseller,
or by contacting the publisher—

Atelier Books, Ltd.
1224 Vallecita Drive
Santa Fe, NM, USA 87501.
E-mail: atelierbooks@gmail.com

Other books by the author

2008 Indigo

2008 Wait Here I Have Gone To Get Help

2008 AmericaAmerica When Will You See

2008 Why New Mexicans Love New Mexico

2008 Timeless People in a Changing Time

2008 Remembrances of Things to Come

2005 100 Artists of the Southwest

2003 100 Artists of the West Coast

2001 The Chania Town News

2000 Fashion Asia

2000 The Food of Sri Lanka

2000 Periplus Map of Sri Lanka

1999 *Dhaba:* The Street Food of India

1998 Preparing for E-Commerce in Asia

1997 India's Consumer Market

1997 Doing Business in Today's India

1996 The Cultural Climate of Sri Lanka

1996 A Soul You Can See

1994 The *Mahavamsa* of Sri Lanka

1994 Painting the Buddha's Eyes

1989 Crystals

1988 Not By Bread Alone

1987 California Fashion Designers

1982 Fifty West Coast Artists

1980 Serenissim and Exciplex

1979 Telephone Call

1974 America Explored (editor)

Printed in the United States
R3488100001B/R34881PG203966BVX1B/1-3/P